About Me: Chris T. Risen

Hello and welcome! I'm Chris T. Risen, a seasoned professional with an extensive background in direct marketing, affiliate marketing, sales funnels, and leading dynamic sales teams. With years of invaluable experience under my belt, I've had the privilege of being a partner in one of the esteemed organizations recognized on the Inc 500 list of fastest-growing companies.

Professional Background

My journey in the dynamic field of marketing began over a decade ago, where my innate passion for connecting products with people found its true calling. Over the years, I have dedicated my skills and effort to marketing, where I've worked tirelessly to understand the intricacies and nuances that drive successful campaigns.

I've spearheaded marketing initiatives for eight distinctive brands, each with its unique identity, audience, and market position. This diversity in experience has not only broadened my perspective but also deepened my insights into the multifaceted world of marketing, making me adaptable and proficient in handling various marketing challenges and opportunities.

Expertise

Direct Marketing: With a robust background in direct marketing, I've developed and executed campaigns that directly engage the target audience, driving response and conversions through carefully crafted strategies and messages.

Affiliate Marketing: In the realm of affiliate marketing, I've worked on both sides of the spectrum—promoting products as an affiliate and driving sales through affiliates. This comprehensive experience has provided me with a deep understanding of the affiliate marketing landscape.

Sales Funnels: Mastering the art and science of sales funnels, I've successfully created and optimized conversion-focused funnels that not only attract but also retain customers, maximizing lifetime value and enhancing customer satisfaction.

Sales Teams: Leading high-performance sales teams has been one of my areas of expertise. By fostering a collaborative and motivated environment, I've guided teams to exceed sales targets while maintaining a focus on providing value to our clients and customers.

Inc 500 Fastest Growing Company Partnership: Being a partner in an Inc 500 recognized company has been a monumental milestone in my career. It is a testament to the collective hard work, innovation, and relentless pursuit of excellence that defines my approach to business and marketing.

My Approach

I approach marketing as a dynamic, evolving field that requires a blend of creativity, analytics, and an unerring focus on customer needs. In every campaign, strategy, or project I undertake, the customer is always at the core. By understanding their needs, preferences, and behaviors, I craft marketing strategies that resonate, engage, and convert.

Here's to successful marketing endeavors and the exciting journey that each campaign brings. Looking forward to crossing paths with like-minded professionals, collaborators, and enthusiasts in the field!

Chris T. Risen

Introduction: Navigating The Digital Landscape

In the digital age, the term "social media marketing" has become a buzzword, frequently tossed around in business meetings, seminars, and casual coffee shop conversations. But what does it truly mean, and more importantly, why is it vital for contemporary businesses?

Social media marketing is the art and science of promoting products, services, or brands on platforms where people socially connect, share, and communicate. From Facebook and Instagram to Twitter and LinkedIn, these platforms aren't just for posting vacation photos or connecting with old friends. They've transformed into powerful business tools, bringing brands closer to their audiences in ways previously unimaginable.

Why the emphasis on social media marketing? For starters, it's where the audience is. With billions of users worldwide, social media platforms offer unparalleled access to potential customers, clients, and fans. Moreover, it's not just about quantity; it's about quality. Social media provides a unique opportunity for brands to engage in two-way dialogues with their audiences, fostering relationships that are more personal and genuine than traditional advertising channels.

This guide's purpose is clear and simple: to demystify the vast world of social media marketing for beginners. Whether you're a small business owner hoping to expand your online presence, a marketer looking to enhance your skills, or a novice just curious about the digital realm, this guide is crafted for you. Dive in, and let's embark on this journey together, simplifying the complexities of social media marketing and uncovering its potential for success.

Chapter 1: Understanding Social Media Marketing

Definition and Overview

Social media marketing (SMM) is a multifaceted approach to digital marketing that employs various social media platforms to achieve communication and branding goals. It's about leveraging these platforms to connect with your audience, build your brand, increase sales, and drive website traffic. Social media marketing involves publishing great content on your profiles, listening to and engaging with your followers, analyzing results, and running social media advertisements.

Social media platforms allow users to interact with each other and create and share content. In SMM, companies can use these platforms to engage with their customers, prospects, and a wider audience. Every social media platform is unique, having distinct features, styles of interaction, and types of audiences. Understanding these nuances is key to effectively using social media for marketing.

Importance in Today's Digital Age

In our interconnected, digital world, social media plays a critical role in shaping people's perceptions and influencing their behaviors. According to data from the Pew Research Center, as of 2021, about 72% of the public uses some form of social media. With such a vast user base, businesses have the opportunity to connect with a global audience, irrespective of industry, size, or geography.

Here's why SMM is indispensable in the digital age:

1. **Unprecedented Reach:** Social media platforms house billions of active users. For businesses, this means access to a vast and diverse audience, from local communities to global markets.
2. **Cost-Effective**: Many features of social media marketing

are free. Businesses can create profiles, post content, and interact with users without spending a dime. Paid advertising options, while available, are often less expensive than traditional advertising channels.

3. **Targeted Marketing**: Advanced targeting options allow businesses to reach specific demographics, making campaigns more efficient and effective.

Potential Benefits for Businesses

Businesses that effectively leverage social media marketing can reap numerous benefits, including but not limited to:

- **Brand Awareness:** Social media is a great way to introduce people to a new brand or remind them about an existing brand. With the right strategy, businesses can quickly increase their visibility and recognition.
- **Community Building:** Beyond individual transactions, social media allows brands to build communities. These platforms foster engagement and interaction, creating loyal customers and brand advocates.
- **Lead Generation:** Businesses can use social media to attract and capture new leads, ultimately driving sales and revenue.
- **Customer Service and Feedback:** Social media provides an instant channel for customer service and feedback, allowing businesses to address concerns, answer questions, and build goodwill in real-time.
- **Insights and Analysis:** With powerful analytics tools, businesses can gain insights into their audience's behaviors and preferences, helping them to make data-driven decisions and optimize their strategies.

Through its myriad features and wide-reaching appeal, social media marketing emerges as a cornerstone of effective digital marketing in the 21st century. For businesses seeking to navigate and thrive in the online sphere, understanding and harnessing the power of social media marketing is non-negotiable. This guide is your ally in this endeavor, providing you with the knowledge and tools needed to embark on a successful social media marketing journey. Whether you're a seasoned professional or a digital marketing neophyte, there's something here for everyone. Welcome to the dynamic, ever-evolving world of social media marketing!

Chapter 2: Setting Marketing Goals

Importance of Setting Goals

Before embarking on the social media marketing journey, it's essential to establish clear, concise goals. Establishing goals provides direction and purpose for your marketing efforts, acting as the compass guiding your strategies and tactics. Without explicit objectives, you risk wandering aimlessly in the digital landscape without measuring success or failure effectively.

The importance of setting goals lies in their ability to provide focus. With a set target, businesses can align their resources and efforts towards achieving specific outcomes. Goals also facilitate measurement and analysis, allowing you to track performance and make necessary adjustments to your strategies in real-time. Ultimately, setting goals maximizes the efficiency and efficacy of your marketing efforts, ensuring a higher return on investment.

SMART Goals Framework

The SMART framework is a popular tool used for goal setting, providing structure and guidance during the planning process. Here's a quick breakdown of the acronym:

- **Specific:** Goals should be clear, concise, and well-defined. Vague or generalized goals are unhelpful because they don't provide sufficient direction.
- **Measurable:** You must be able to track and measure the progress and outcomes of your goals. Without a metric for measurement, it is impossible to ascertain success or failure.
- **Achievable**: Goals should be realistic and attainable. While it's important to set challenging targets, they must be reachable and plausible to motivate your team.
- **Relevant:** Each goal should align with your broader business objectives and be pertinent to the key drivers of

success in your industry.

- **Time-bound:** Goals need a timeline. Setting a deadline ensures urgency and commitment, promoting a focused approach to achieving the targets.

Examples of Social Media Marketing Goals

Below are examples of SMART goals in the context of social media marketing:

Increase Brand Awareness:

- Specific: Increase our brand's visibility and engagement rate on social media.
- Measurable: Achieve a 20% increase in the number of followers and a 15% higher engagement rate.
- Achievable: Use consistent posting, engaging content, and social media ads.
- Relevant: Higher brand visibility will lead to more inquiries and sales.
- Time-bound: Achieve this in the next six months.

Drive Traffic to Website:

- Specific: Increase the amount of social media referral traffic to the website.
- Measurable: Achieve a 30% increase in social media-driven website visits.
- Achievable: Share engaging content with clear calls-to-action and links to the website.
- Relevant: More website traffic can lead to higher conversion rates.
- Time-bound: Achieve this target in the next quarter.

Generate Leads:

- Specific: Use social media platforms to capture new leads.
- Measurable: Collect 200 new leads per month from social media campaigns.
- Achievable: Implement lead generation campaigns on platforms like Facebook and LinkedIn.

- Relevant: New leads are crucial for sales and business growth.
- Time-bound: Start immediately with a review and analysis after three months.

These examples serve as templates for creating your social media marketing goals. Remember, the SMART framework is flexible, and your goals will depend on your business's unique needs and circumstances. Whether you're aiming to increase brand awareness, drive traffic, or generate leads, setting SMART goals is the starting point of a successful social media marketing strategy. Armed with clear objectives, you can move forward with confidence, crafting campaigns that resonate with your audience and drive meaningful results. Happy planning!

Chapter 3: Identifying Your Audience

Explanation of Target Audience

At its core, your target audience comprises the individuals most likely to be interested in your product, service, or message. They're not just any random users online; they're the subset of the digital populace whose needs, wants, or interests align with what you offer. Effectively, they're the cornerstone of your social media marketing strategy, influencing your content, advertising decisions, and engagement methods.

Importance of Knowing Your Audience

Understanding your audience is paramount for several reasons:

1. **Tailored Content:** When you know your audience, you can create content that speaks directly to their interests, values, and pain points.
2. **Efficient Spending:** Knowledge about your audience ensures that any paid promotions or advertisements reach those most likely to convert, ensuring optimal return on investment.
3. **Building Relationships:** Authentic and lasting brand relationships are cultivated when you understand and cater to your audience's needs and preferences.
4. **Feedback Loop:** An understanding of your audience fosters better communication, enabling a feedback mechanism that can drive business growth and innovation.

How to Identify and Understand Your Audience

To navigate the vast ocean of social media users and pinpoint your audience, consider the following steps:

1. Analyze Existing Customers: Look at who's already buying from you. What do they have in common? Their demographics, behaviors, and feedback can offer significant clues about your broader audience.

2. Competitor Insights: Examine the audience of your competitors. While you shouldn't copy their strategy, understanding who they target can provide valuable insights.
3. Engage and Listen: Interact with your followers. Ask questions, conduct surveys, or start discussions. The more you engage, the more you'll learn about them.
4. Social Media Analytics: Platforms like Facebook and Twitter offer built-in analytics tools. Dive into these analytics to understand the demographics, interests, and behaviors of your followers.
5. Stay Updated: Remember, audience preferences and behaviors evolve. Regularly reassess and adjust your understanding of your audience.

Creating Customer Personas

One of the most effective ways to visualize and understand your target audience is by creating customer personas. A persona is a semi-fictional representation of your ideal customer, based on market research and real data about your existing customers.

To craft a customer persona:

1. **Demographic Information:** Age, gender, income level, education, occupation, etc.
2. **Psychographic Information:** Interests, hobbies, values, pain points, and buying motivations.
3. **Media Preferences:** Where do they spend their time online? Which social platforms do they prefer? What types of content engage them?
4. **Behavioral Insights:** Buying habits, brand interactions, and product usage.
5. **Personal Background:** This can include elements like family status, lifestyle, or life stage.

Once you've gathered this data, synthesize it into a coherent profile. For instance:

"Sarah, a 30-year-old urban professional with a penchant for sustainable living. She's tech-savvy, often browses Instagram and Pinterest, and is motivated by eco-friendly brands that share her values. She's likely to invest in quality over quantity and is often the go-to 'tech guru' in her circle."

Having such personas at hand allows marketers to empathize with and tailor strategies to their audience. If you cater to multiple audience segments, create multiple personas. These profiles serve as a touchstone, ensuring your marketing efforts remain targeted and effective.

In conclusion, understanding your audience is the foundation upon which successful social media marketing strategies are built. By recognizing their preferences, needs, and behaviors, businesses can craft compelling narratives, foster authentic connections, and drive meaningful results. In the subsequent chapters, we'll delve into leveraging this understanding for tangible success in the digital realm.

Chapter 4: Choosing The Right Platforms

Overview of Popular Social Media Platforms

With the digital age booming, numerous social media platforms have emerged, each offering unique features and catering to distinct audiences. Here's a brief overview of some of the most popular ones:

1. **Facebook:** A universal platform with over 2.8 billion users as of early 2022, Facebook is ideal for businesses of all types. It offers versatile features including pages, groups, events, and paid advertising.
2. **Instagram:** A visual-centric platform, particularly popular among millennials and Gen Z. It's ideal for brands with visually appealing products or services.
3. **Twitter:** Known for real-time updates, Twitter is great for brands looking to engage in immediate conversations, share news, or provide customer service.
4. **LinkedIn:** A professional network, LinkedIn is crucial for B2B companies, professionals seeking to build industry connections, and brands looking to hire.
5. **Pinterest:** A visual discovery engine where users find inspiration, Pinterest is particularly effective for sectors like fashion, decor, arts, and crafts.
6. **TikTok:** A short-form video platform that's seen a rapid rise in popularity, especially among younger audiences.
7. **YouTube:** The premier video-sharing platform, perfect for brands with video content ranging from tutorials to advertisements.

Choosing the Right Platform for Your Business

The right platform for your business largely depends on where your target audience spends their time and the nature of your content. Here's a guideline to help you decide:

1. **Identify Your Audience:** As discussed in Chapter 3,

knowing your audience is paramount. For instance, if you're targeting professionals in a B2B setup, LinkedIn might be more effective than TikTok.

2. **Content Type:** If your content is visually appealing, platforms like Instagram or Pinterest might be suitable. On the other hand, if you have longer video content, YouTube is the way to go.

3. **Engagement Level:** Some platforms, like Twitter, demand higher levels of real-time engagement than platforms like LinkedIn.

4. **Resources:** Managing a social media account requires resources, especially time. Ensure you choose platforms that you can manage effectively, rather than spreading yourself too thin.

5. **Analyze Competitors:** Where are your competitors? Analyzing their presence and effectiveness on platforms can provide valuable insights.

Pros and Cons of Different Platforms

Facebook:

- Pros: Universal audience, versatile content options, robust advertising tools.
- Cons: Declining organic reach, saturated with content, younger users migrating to newer platforms.

Instagram:

- Pros: High engagement rates, visual storytelling, and shopping features.
- Cons: Requires high-quality visuals, primarily mobile-centric, competition for visibility.

Twitter:

- Pros: Real-time engagement, concise content, ability to tap into trending topics.
- Cons: Limited content length, short lifespan of tweets, potential for negative interactions.

LinkedIn:

- Pros: Professional audience, B2B networking, organic reach still viable.
- Cons: Less casual and spontaneous, not ideal for all business types, lower daily user rates compared to other platforms.

Pinterest:

- Pros: High purchase intent from users, lasting content lifespan, visual discovery.
- Cons: Niche audience, requires constant pinning for visibility.

TikTok:

- Pros: Rapidly growing user base, high engagement, innovative content format.
- Cons:Skews towards younger demographic, content can be hit-or-miss, potential geopolitical concerns.

YouTube:

- Pros: Dominant video platform, long content lifespan, monetization opportunities.
- Cons: Requires high-quality videos, saturated in popular niches, demands consistent posting.

Conclusion

Choosing the right platforms is a balancing act between understanding where your audience is and leveraging the unique features of each platform. Remember, it's not about being everywhere but being impactful where you choose to be. Focus on platforms that align with your business objectives, resonate with your audience, and complement the nature of your content. This chapter serves as a starting point, but as the digital landscape evolves, always be ready to re-evaluate and adapt your platform choices.

Chapter 5: Crafting Compelling Content

Types of Content for Social Media

Content is the lifeblood of social media marketing. Here are some predominant types to consider:

1. **Images:** Still photos showcasing products, behind-the-scenes looks, infographics, and more.
2. **Videos:** From short video clips on platforms like TikTok to longer explainer videos on YouTube, visual storytelling is powerful.
3. **Blog Posts & Articles**: Sharing your latest blog posts or industry-related news can drive traffic to your website.
4. **User-Generated Content (UGC):** Sharing content your users or customers create about your products or services.
5. **Polls & Surveys:** Engage with your audience by gauging their opinions.
6. **Stories:** Temporary content (like Instagram or Facebook Stories) that allows for more casual, spontaneous sharing.
7. **Live Streams:** Real-time streaming on platforms like Facebook, Instagram, or YouTube can be used for events, Q&As, or product launches.

Tips for Creating Engaging Content

1. Know Your Audience: As reiterated, always keep your target audience in mind. What are their interests, preferences, and pain points?
2. Be Authentic: People appreciate genuineness. Share your business's story, its ups and downs, and its human side.
3. Use Storytelling: Instead of hard-selling, narrate a story. Stories are relatable, memorable, and engaging.
4. Stay Relevant & Updated: Keep up with current events, trends, and holidays. But always ensure relevance to your brand before jumping on a trend.
5. Encourage Interaction: Ask questions, initiate polls, or use

call-to-actions to get your audience involved.

6. Maintain Consistency: While it's essential to keep content varied, maintaining a consistent brand voice and style is crucial.

Importance of Visuals and Multimedia

We live in a visual era. The brain processes visual information 60,000 times faster than text. Here's why visuals are paramount:

1. **Attention Grabbing:** In a cluttered feed, striking visuals can make users stop and look.
2. **Enhanced Understanding:** Complex information can be simplified using infographics or videos.
3. **Emotional Connection:** Visuals can evoke emotions, making your content more impactful.
4. **Higher Engagement:** Content with visuals often gets more likes, shares, and comments.
5. **Diverse Content**: Multimedia like GIFs, videos, or interactive content can break the monotony and keep the audience engaged.

Content Calendar and Scheduling

Planning ahead is the key to maintaining consistency and ensuring diverse content. Here's where a content calendar comes in handy:

1. **Organization:** Outline what content will be published and when, allowing for a clear visual representation of your content strategy over weeks or months.
2. **Diverse Content:** By planning, you can ensure that your content is varied, alternating between images, videos, blogs, etc.
3. **Timely Posting:** Recognize important dates, holidays, or events relevant to your brand and schedule content accordingly.
4. **Resource Allocation:** Knowing your content plan in advance helps in allocating resources, be it for content creation, design, or promotion.

5. **Tools & Platforms:** Use tools like Buffer, Hootsuite, or Sprout Social to schedule and automate your content posting.

Conclusion

Crafting compelling content isn't just about posting regularly; it's about posting content that resonates. Quality always trumps quantity. By understanding your audience, leveraging the power of visuals, and staying organized with a content calendar, you set the stage for a successful social media strategy. In the following chapters, we'll delve deeper into optimizing this content for maximum impact.

Chapter 6: Engaging With Your Audience

In the realm of social media marketing, broadcasting your message isn't enough. The power of these platforms lies in their ability to foster two-way communication. Engagement is the bridge between a brand and its audience, turning passive viewers into active participants and, eventually, loyal customers.

Importance of Engagement

1. **Builds Trust:** Regular and genuine interaction with your audience humanizes your brand. It shows there are real people behind the brand who care about customers' needs and feedback.
2. **Increases Reach:** Platforms like Facebook and Instagram often prioritize content with higher engagement, making your posts more likely to appear in users' feeds.
3. **Feedback Loop:** Engaging with your audience provides immediate feedback, allowing you to understand what's resonating and what's not.
4. **Fosters Loyalty:** A brand that actively listens and responds to its audience is more likely to cultivate a loyal customer base.

How to Effectively Communicate with Your Audience

1. **Be Proactive:** Don't just wait for comments or questions. Initiate discussions, ask questions, and create content that encourages interaction.
2. **Respond Promptly:** If someone takes the time to comment or ask a question, prioritize responding in a timely manner.
3. **Stay Authentic:** Automated responses can come off as insincere. Ensure your replies are genuine and personalized.
4. **Use Stories & Polls:** Features like Instagram Stories or Twitter polls are interactive by nature. They're excellent tools for direct engagement.

5. **Host AMAs (Ask Me Anything):** Platforms like Reddit or Instagram make it easy to host Q&A sessions, allowing for direct and candid conversations with your audience.
6. **Utilize User-Generated Content:** Showcase content created by your users or customers, making them feel valued and heard.

Managing Negative Feedback and Criticism

Encountering negative feedback or criticism is inevitable. However, how a brand responds can make all the difference. Here are some tips:

1. **Stay Calm:** It's easy to react defensively, especially if the feedback feels unjust. However, it's crucial to approach the situation calmly and professionally.
2. **Acknowledge & Apologize:** If a mistake was made on your part, acknowledge it and apologize sincerely.
3. **Offer Solutions:** If a user has had a bad experience, offer a tangible solution or way to make it right.
4. **Take the Conversation Offline:** For detailed issues, consider moving the conversation to a private channel like Direct Message or email.
5. **Learn & Improve:** Instead of dismissing criticism outright, see if there are valid points that can be used as feedback for improvement.
6. **Know When to Disengage**: Some comments or users may be trolling or looking for a reaction. Recognize when it's more appropriate to disengage or, if needed, block excessively disruptive users.

Conclusion

Engagement is the heart and soul of social media marketing. It's more than just a metric; it's a testament to the relationship between a brand and its audience. By prioritizing genuine engagement, brands can foster trust, loyalty, and community. It's not just about responding but about understanding, empathizing, and growing through continuous interaction. As we navigate further into the intricacies of social media marketing in subsequent chapters, remember: behind every like, comment, or share, there's a person seeking a genuine connection.

Chapter 7: Utilizing Paid Advertising

The vast world of social media provides an impressive organic reach, but as these platforms evolve, the landscape becomes increasingly competitive. Here's where paid advertising comes into play, offering brands the opportunity to amplify their message, target specific audiences, and achieve tangible results.

Overview of Paid Social Advertising

Paid social advertising involves promoting your content through sponsored ads on social media platforms. Unlike organic reach, where you rely on non-paid strategies to show your content to users, paid ads ensure your content is displayed to a specific audience, based on various targeting criteria.

Key components of paid social advertising include:

1. **Ad Formats:** From simple image or text ads to carousels, video ads, and immersive full-screen experiences.
2. **Targeting:** Define who sees your ads based on demographics, interests, behavior, location, and more.
3. **Placement:** Where your ad appears, be it in feeds, stories, sidebars, or in between user content.
4. **Budgeting:** How much you're willing to spend, which can be set as a daily or lifetime budget.
5. **Bidding:** The amount you're willing to pay for a user to interact with your ad, whether through views, clicks, or other actions.

When and Why to Use Paid Advertising

1. **Amplified Reach**: While organic strategies have their merit, paid ads ensure your content reaches beyond your immediate followers or organic discovery.
2. **Targeted Exposure:** Paid ads allow precision targeting, ensuring your content is seen by users most likely to be interested.
3. **Event Promotion:** If you have a time-sensitive event or

sale, paid ads can provide the necessary immediate boost.

4. **New Product Launch:** Introduce a new product or service to a wider audience or retarget previous customers.
5. **Competitive Landscape:** In saturated industries, paid ads can give you an edge over competitors.
6. **Measurable ROI:** Every aspect of paid advertising is trackable, from views and clicks to conversions, allowing a clear view of return on investment.

How to Set Up and Optimize Ads

1. **Clear Objectives:** Before starting, define what you aim to achieve. Be it brand awareness, lead generation, conversions, or engagement, having a clear goal is crucial.
2. **Platform Selection:** Choose a platform aligned with your target audience and objectives. For instance, Instagram might be more suitable for a fashion brand, while LinkedIn caters to B2B audiences.
3. **Audience Segmentation:** Instead of targeting everyone, segment your audience. Create different ads for different demographic or interest groups for higher relevancy.
4. **Ad Design:** Ensure your ad visuals and copy align with your brand and resonate with your target audience. A/B test different versions to see which performs best.
5. **Optimal Budgeting:** Start with a moderate budget, analyze performance, and adjust accordingly. It's essential to optimize for cost-effectiveness.
6. **Monitor and Adjust:** Use in-built analytics tools to monitor ad performance. Regularly adjust based on feedback, ensuring your ads remain effective and relevant.

Conclusion

Paid advertising is a potent tool in the arsenal of social media marketing. When executed correctly, it offers a strategic avenue to achieve specific business goals, from brand visibility to tangible sales. It's essential to approach it with a mix of creativity, strategy, and analysis, always keeping the end-user in mind. As with all aspects of social media marketing, success in paid advertising is a blend of art and science. As we further delve into advanced strategies in the coming chapters, remember: in the digital age, adaptability and learning are the keys to ongoing success.

Chapter 8: Measuring And Analyzing Performance

A strategic approach to social media marketing isn't just about crafting and delivering content; it's also about understanding the impact of your efforts. By measuring and analyzing your performance, you can make data-driven decisions, optimize your strategies, and continually enhance your ROI.

Importance of Analytics

1. **Informed Decisions:** Analytics offer a clear picture of what's working and what isn't, enabling brands to allocate resources more effectively.
2. **Understand Your Audience:** Analytical data provides insights into your audience's behaviors, preferences, and interactions with your content.
3. **Achieve Business Goals:** By tracking key metrics, you can align your social media strategies with broader business objectives.
4. **Optimization:** Regular analysis allows for real-time adjustments, ensuring strategies remain relevant and impactful.
5. **Competitive Analysis:** Understand where you stand in comparison to competitors and identify market gaps or opportunities.

Overview of Key Performance Indicators (KPI's)

KPIs are specific metrics used to track the progress toward a defined goal. Some essential social media KPI's include:

1. **Engagement Rate:** Measures the level of interaction content receives. It can include likes, shares, comments, and more.
2. **Reach and Impressions:** Reach denotes the total number of unique users who've seen your content, while impressions refer to the number of times your content was displayed, irrespective of clicks.

3. **Click-Through Rate (CTR):** This indicates the percentage of users who clicked on a link in your content.
4. **Conversion Rate:** Of the users who clicked through, how many took a desired action, like making a purchase or signing up for a newsletter?
5. **Follower Growth Rate:** How quickly is your audience on social platforms growing?
6. **Brand Mention:** How often is your brand mentioned or discussed across social platforms?
7. **Customer Testimonials and Reviews:** Positive feedback and ratings from customers shared on social platforms.
8. **ROI:** The return on investment calculates the financial return relative to the amount spent on a campaign or advertisement.

Tools for Tracking and Analyzing Performance

There's a myriad of tools available to assist with tracking and analyzing performance:

1. **Platform-Specific Insights:**
   - Facebook Insights: Provides data on page likes, post reach, engagement, and more.
   - Instagram Insights: Offers metrics on follower demographics, post reach, and profile views.
   - Twitter Analytics: Details on tweet impressions, engagement rate, and follower growth.
2. **Google Analytics:** Particularly useful for tracking website traffic originating from social media and understanding user behavior once they land on your site.
3. **Hootsuite:** A social media management tool that also offers comprehensive analytics and custom reports.
4. **Buffer:** Alongside scheduling content, Buffer provides insights into post performance and audience engagement.
5. **Socialbakers:** A unified social media marketing platform that offers AI-powered insights, competitor analysis, and audience understanding.
6. **Sprout Social:** Provides detailed analytics on audience

engagement, publishing behavior, and performance comparison tools.

Conclusion

In the evolving landscape of social media marketing, the old adage, "what gets measured gets managed," rings truer than ever. By prioritizing performance measurement and analysis, brands can ensure their strategies remain agile, effective, and aligned with overarching business objectives. It's not just about numbers, but about deriving actionable insights from these numbers to craft stories of success. As we progress further into the intricacies of social media marketing in upcoming chapters, remember that behind every statistic is a narrative waiting to be uncovered. Your task is to decode it.

Conclusion

Congratulations on completing "A Beginner's Guide to Social Media Marketing: Made Simple!" Through the various chapters, you've been equipped with foundational knowledge and insights necessary for launching your social media marketing journey.

Let's revisit the key takeaways:

1. **Understanding Social Media Marketing**: Recognizing that social media marketing is pivotal for brand visibility and engagement in the digital age. It's not just about being online; it's about being present and active with a strategy in place.
2. **Setting Marketing Goals**: The importance of establishing clear, SMART goals cannot be overstated. They act as your guiding stars, helping align your strategies for effective results.
3. **Identifying Your Audience:** A deep understanding of your audience informs your content strategy, allowing for personalized, relevant, and engaging interactions.
4. **Choosing the Right Platforms:** With myriad social platforms available, selecting the ones that resonate with your audience and business objectives is crucial.
5. **Crafting Compelling Content:** Quality content is king. It's vital to produce content that not only reflects your brand but also captivates and adds value to your audience.
6. **Engaging with Your Audience:** Active engagement helps in building a community around your brand, fostering trust, loyalty, and brand advocacy.
7. **Utilizing Paid Advertising:** Leveraging paid ads amplifies your reach, targets precisely, and enhances your brand's presence, driving tangible results.
8. **Measuring and Analyzing Performance:** Consistently tracking and analyzing your performance informs your

strategy, facilitating a process of continuous learning and improvement.

As you stand at the precipice of your social media marketing adventure, it's important to acknowledge that the digital landscape is ever-evolving. While this guide provides you with the fundamentals, social media marketing is a dynamic field. Successful marketers are those who are adaptable, curious, and always willing to learn. It's about trying, testing, failing, learning, and trying again.

Embarking on social media marketing might seem daunting, but remember that every expert was once a beginner. With the foundational principles in hand, you're well-prepared to navigate the dynamic waters of social media. Implement the strategies shared, stay updated with the latest trends, and most importantly, don't be afraid to experiment.

As you initiate your journey, embrace the excitement and challenges that come with it. With each post, ad, and engagement, you're not only marketing but also building relationships and creating value. Here's to your success in crafting a compelling social media presence and achieving your marketing goals!

Thank you for choosing this guide as your starting point. The world of social media awaits, and it's yours to explore and conquer. Happy marketing!